This is Calmer

Inspiration, support and encouragement
for the entrepreneurial mind

Tania Diggory

The Comfortable Book Co.

A special thank you

Luke, for every moment since Passing Clouds.

The Diggory clan, for your love, support
and unwavering belief.

I wouldn't be where I am today without you all.

Longevity, Ellie and Emma, for enabling this idea
to become a reality and helping me bring this book
into existence. For this, I'm eternally grateful.

Murray, Roy and Mark, for your time,
guidance and feedback.

My mentors, for always having my back.
I continue to learn so much from you all.

First published in 2017 by The Comfortable Book Co.

Design by Longevity
Illustration by Ellie Wilkinson
Editing by Emma Hypher

Diggory, Tania, 1986 - author.
/ This Is Calmer : Inspiration, support and encouragement for the entrepreneurial mind.

ISBN: 978-1-9999013-0-1

Contents

Introduction

As an entrepreneur, you take big risks to make your dreams a reality. Pursuing a purpose you believe in and seeing the results of your hard work come to fruition can bring invaluable rewards. But it's inevitable you'll encounter some challenges along the way. How do you manage feelings of anxiety, uncertainty or overwhelm while running a business?

I have learnt that preparing your mindset for this lifestyle and nurturing it on a daily basis is essential for your long-term success.

I use the words 'management' and 'managing' throughout this book, as I believe creating a business-life balance is a process that takes a bit of work. It comes from understanding yourself and learning how to nurture your emotional wellbeing effectively – particularly when challenges arise.

The first chapter – 'Managing your wellbeing' – explores the idea that the entrepreneurial journey ultimately starts with you and your mindset. Use this chapter as a source of support, insight and tips for looking after your mind on a daily basis, and giving yourself the best chance of startup success.

Next up, 'Managing your startup' delves into the key components of setting yourself up for entrepreneurial life and building the foundations needed to succeed. A lot of this stems from personal experience, learning the key components needed to scale a business, as well as supporting other entrepreneurs.

Finally, 'Managing your relationships' looks at a crucial aspect of developing any business. Whether it's your team, customers, partners or anybody else connected to your work, this chapter explores how building relationships has the power to nurture and grow your business – as well as providing you with valuable support along your journey.

These three key areas have been fundamental to the success of my entrepreneurial journey so far, and it is my hope that this management model inspires you to approach your business in a way that places your mental health and happiness at the heart of what you do.

I believe we should never feel ashamed of the struggles we go through as entrepreneurs to achieve our goals – it takes courage to live this lifestyle. May this book give you peace of mind that you're not alone on this journey and provide you with the support and encouragement you need while running your business.

I hope it inspires you to move toward your dreams with increased clarity, confidence and bravery.

Chapter One:
Managing your wellbeing

Daily inspiration to nurture your mindset

Starting up your own independent business, enterprise or project takes courage, perseverance and bravery.

Remind yourself of this every day.

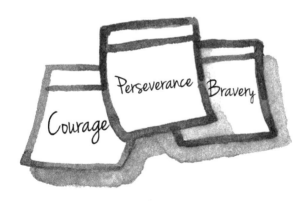

It's exciting that you feel inspired to make your dreams a reality, because your ideas are unique to you and your vision won't be like anyone else's.

No one in the entire world is like you, therefore being yourself is your biggest strength and asset. Embrace what makes you 'you' and let that be reflected through your business.

Take time to understand yourself, your strengths and what makes you happy as best you can. Be comfortable with your whole self and know that who you are, and what you are doing, is enough.

Recommended viewing:
Neil Pasricha's TED Talk, *'The 3 A's of awesome'*

The entrepreneurial journey can feel all-consuming and as much as it's important to work hard to achieve your goals, it's equally as important to take time out to reflect, recharge and assess how things are going.

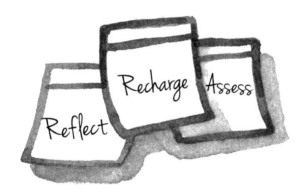

Ask yourself these questions on a regular basis:

- How do I feel?
- What seems to be working well and which areas may need improving?
- How might I go about that and who may be able to help me?

Reflection is an essential component of running your business. Listen to your intuition.

Maintaining a healthy lifestyle and exercise is a vital part of your wellbeing as an entrepreneur.

Finding a work-life balance can be challenging when running a business – remember that taking a bit of time out each week for leisure and self-development can boost your productivity, enhance creativity and keep you feeling centred. Your health is your number one priority.

It's easy to compare yourself to others. However, every person on this planet is different – we all live through different experiences and circumstances - so remember that your experiences are unique.

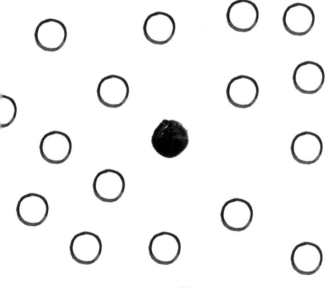

Daily work on self-development, confidence and belief in your vision can only enhance the experience of your startup journey. Find out what works for you – whether it's through joining a group or a network of like-minded people, reading inspirational and informative books, or listening to renowned speakers in your field – and allocate time each week to your own personal development.

Recommended reading:
Elizabeth Gilbert's book, *Big Magic*

Be open to learning from the experiences of others who have walked the entrepreneurial path. The ability to learn valuable lessons from your peers and utilise it to enhance your journey is a key strength of entrepreneurs. We never stop learning.

Take time each day to write down three things you are grateful for, whether it's something that's happened in your business, a positive influence in your life or something else entirely.

Recognising how you feel each day and acknowledging positive outcomes in your busy life are essential to managing your wellbeing.

If you feel anxious, try to accept that feeling without any self-judgement. Tell yourself that the feeling is temporary, breathe slowly and deeply (in through your nose and out through your mouth) and keep doing so until you start to feel calmer.

Recommended reading:
'How to improve your mental wellbeing' at
www.mind.org.uk/information-support/
tips-for-everyday-living/wellbeing/

You are capable of handling whatever comes your way, possibly more than you give yourself credit for.

Recommended reading:
Susan Jeffers' book, Feel the Fear and Do It Anyway

Stepping out of your comfort zone enables you to realise what you're truly capable of achieving. You have one life – what's the best that could happen if you try?

The entrepreneurial lifestyle doesn't resonate with everyone, so if you feel this is a calling for you then embrace the opportunity with all your heart. Be brave.

Recommended viewing:
Tim Ferriss' TED Talk, *'Why you should define your fears instead of your goals'*

Facing and learning from challenges

Particularly in the early years of running your business, it's common to come across challenges. If being a successful entrepreneur was so easy, everyone would be doing it – take comfort in that and know that it takes courage to do what you're doing.

It's natural that every aspect of how your business functions will feel magnified to you as you're so invested in it. When you face a challenge or something unexpected, tell yourself, "This too shall pass" – and know that you'll handle it to the best of your ability.

Poor communication and misunderstandings are the root causes of many issues in business. Every person absorbs and interprets situations differently; we each have our own needs and ways of filtering information. It helps to remember this before jumping to any conclusions.

Recommended reading:
Professor Steve Peters book, *The Chimp Paradox: The Mind Management Programme For Confidence, Success and Happiness*

We've all been there – having to deal with confrontation is hardly an enjoyable experience. However, it's inevitable it will crop up when running your own business, so it's in your best interest to work on your approach to facing challenges early on.

When faced with confrontation, remember there is a difference between compromising to meet someone halfway, and compromising your values and what you believe in – the latter must always be avoided.

It can feel easy to give up when faced with challenges. Through experience, you'll learn the difference between pursuing something that is worth your time and effort, and knowing when you've done all you can before exploring other avenues. If you do end up exploring other avenues, this does not mean you've given up; it means you tried, you did your best and you chose to go down a different route.

When you go through difficult situations, you'll learn about your limits and boundaries, which is crucial for your decision making process.

What's interesting about challenges is they truly test your resilience, perseverance and dedication to achieving your ambitions. Ultimately, you're the only one who can engineer that. Therefore, feel encouraged to take what you learn from each situation and put it into practice.

Putting time aside regularly to review and reflect on your business is key. As your business grows, with each new development ask yourself, "How did that go?" Consider how you contributed to things going well and how you could repeat that in other situations. If things didn't go as you'd expected, what could you do differently in the future?

Recommended viewing:
Jia Jiang's TED Talk,
'What I learned from 100 days of rejection'

Change is a constant in nature and therefore a constant in our lives. How we respond to change is essentially in our control and our reactions can have a significant impact on how we deal with challenging situations.

Evaluate any risks during your startup process and work out what you can do to achieve the best results possible. Do your best to keep calm – there will always be a solution, even if it's not what you'd originally expected. It's another experience you can learn and grow from.

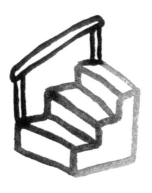

Some of your learning experiences may be difficult to digest, but ultimately they will make you and your business stronger. You may not always see instant benefits, you're creating a strong foundation for personal and professional growth.

Recommended viewing:
Kelly McGonigal's TED Talk,
'How to make stress your friend'

It could be suggested that we grow from our most challenging experiences, even though they can feel painful at the time. Learning from these insights simply adds strings to your bow and builds your armour to face whatever comes your way.

For your overall wellbeing, take time to overcome any challenges you face. It's important to acknowledge your feelings and what you've learnt before moving on. Bring your focus back to thriving on opportunities that do justice to all the hard work you put in. Think about where your energy is best spent.

Be kind to your mind

You've chosen a lifestyle that can present a range
of challenges, places you out of your comfort zone
and truly tests your resilience. Yet it can also provide
incredible, meaningful rewards. Remind yourself of this
every day and acknowledge each of your achievements
along the way.

Achieving longevity in your business requires you to truly look at your mindset on a daily basis. Work towards creating an environment that encourages your personal and professional growth, including your work space and support network.

Recommended reading:
Claire Diaz-Ortiz's book, *Design Your Day*

In your personal time, keep inspirational books, success stories and videos handy that contribute to keeping you on track and remind you of what you're capable of achieving.

As long as you feel you're making progress, even if it's just small amounts, keep persevering and be confident in what you have to offer – because your vision is unique.

Recommended listening:
Dr Wayne Dyer's audio CD, *Inspirational Thoughts*

What you believe about yourself and your business will be reflected in the output of your work. In other words, your brand is an extension of you.

Each time you learn, you evolve and achieve a higher level of understanding yourself and what is important to you.

Failure is not an end point; it is simply a chance to make a positive and productive change, putting into practice the knowledge you've gained from your experiences.

You make your own luck in this world. When you're successful, it is a reflection of your hard work and persistence. Always be prepared and embrace opportunities when they arise.

Be your biggest motivator – if things don't pan out how you thought they would, try not to be too hard on yourself. You are the driving force of your business, and you put in blood, sweat and tears to get to where you are and make it a success. That strength of character is something to be incredibly proud of.

Recommended viewing:
Brené Brown's TED Talk, *'The Power of Vulnerability'*

Take time to recognise the hard work you're applying to make your dreams a reality. Be patient, keep yourself grounded and be proud of every achievement you make.

Recommended viewing:
Andy Puddicombe's TED Talk,
'All it takes is 10 mindful minutes'

Chapter Two:
Managing your startup

Standing out: your leadership qualities

What differentiates one business from another is the leader and visionary behind it.

Not only does being a leader mean that you embrace change, innovate and steer the direction and growth of your business, it's also about how you interact with and inspire people.

Recommended reading:
Robin Sharma's book, *Leadership Wisdom from the Monk Who Sold His Ferrari*

Think about what motivates and energises you. How do you motivate yourself to live your purpose to the full each day and inspire others?

The core foundation of your business is knowing 'why'.
Just as you wouldn't build a house with substandard
tools and materials, you wouldn't build a business that
has a vague strategy with an indecisive framework. Use
your passion and 'why' to create strong foundations to
build your business infrastructure.

Recommended viewing:
Simon Sinek's TED Talk,
'How great leaders inspire action'

Running your own business requires such inner-strength, motivation and determination that your 'why' needs to be nailed down from the very beginning, before any implementation.

On the days that challenge you to keep going, your 'why' will serve as a reminder of your purpose and your mission. It's your reason for pursuing your dream every day.

Consider the values that best represent your business and keep these at the forefront of your mind. This will help you to ensure that any decisions you make about your business align with these values.

Think about how you'd pitch your business to potential customers, investors, partners and clients. In the early stages of your startup, it's important to write out and confidently memorise a brief, persuasive speech to spark interest in what your organisation is about. What makes you and your business unique?

You are the visionary and the heartbeat of your business. Your direction is fundamental to the success of your brand.

Recommended reading:
Stephen R. Covey's book,
The 7 Habits of Highly Effective People

The basics of launching your startup

A business plan enables you to crystallise your thoughts and ambitions. It reaffirms how you intend to build a sustainable and viable business model and encourages you to structure your aims in the most effective way possible.

Just as you mustn't rely on one hard drive to look after all your most important data, you mustn't rely solely on one plan of action to reach your business goals – it's important to be flexible. If Plan A defaults on you, what are you going to do?

What are your backup plans B, C and D? You may well not need to use any of these, but if you experience unexpected turns and Plan A no longer serves the purpose of your business, you may need to adapt and try out another plan. This doesn't change the goal outlined in your business plan, it simply changes the direction to get to your goal.

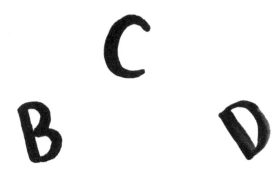

It's likely you'll start your venture wearing many different business hats and taking on various roles to get things moving. There will come a time, however, when you won't physically be able do everything yourself – and rightly so. You're only one person and there's only so much time in a day to do everything you need to do.

If you want your business to run effectively and efficiently, the key is to delegate.

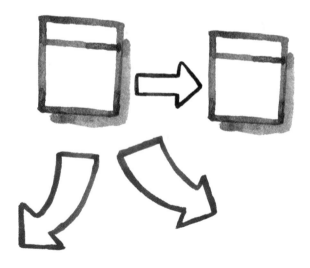

In the early days, take a look at your network and see if you could approach any friends or family to help you out with different areas of expertise, for example marketing, design, accounting, etc. Find out if they could spare a bit of time to help you and contribute to your business – you'd be surprised how many people would be happy to support your vision.

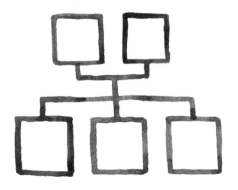

Short-term and long-term goals are both important in order to achieve the big picture of your success.

Consider the idea that building your business has similar traits to raising a child:

Year one: This is about establishing your niche and what makes your business different. Everything feels new, it's the early stages of your long-term plan and it's likely to be rather bumpy. You'll need to look after it and nurture it with everything you've got, every step of the way.

Year two: Your business is beginning to 'have legs' (your baby is now walking) but it still needs a lot of care and attention on your part. You'll also need a great deal of patience and long-term thinking when faced with potential challenges.

Years three to five: These years will feel a lot more independent. You'll have a team in place to support the organisational goals. Your brand will be established. You'll have your business plan in place. While it still needs your attention to detail, you feel more confident in its development and can trust that it's heading in the right direction.

Recommended reading:
'*5 Tips for Profiting During Those Crucial First 5 Years in Business*' at
www.entrepreneur.com/article/247278

Your business is a living entity; just like everything in life, it changes and will need to adapt with the times and trends. Adaptability is a key life skill that will stand you in good stead as an entrepreneur.

Recommended listening:
Gimlet Media's podcast, *'StartUp'*

The problem you are solving for your audience

Before making any decisions around marketing your business, it's essential to work out your target market. All decisions about your products and services are based on knowing your audience and how you can support them.

How does your service provide a solution for your customers? This should be consistent across all your marketing. And rather than a 'hard sell' that's about you, communicate how your business can help them.

Market research is important in the early stages of planning your business. Source as much information as you can to understand your audience's needs, habits and preferences and ensure your product or service meets what they're looking for.

Who is your ideal customer? What is their age, gender and background? What are their interests? What social media channels do they engage with most? The more details you work out, the more authentic your marketing will be as you'll be speaking their language.

Before investing in a new product or service, you can test the idea out on your audience to find out how they respond and what feedback they provide. Not only will this demonstrate your idea is bespoke as you're listening to their needs, it can potentially save you lots of time and money as you'll learn which products and services are worth investing in and which ones to move on from.

Take some time to research organisations you admire or marketing campaigns and adverts that have stood out to you. Look through their online content. Consider what their tone of voice is like as an organisation – how does it make you feel when you engage in their content? Is it friendly? Direct? Humorous?

Be consistent in your language, tone of voice and what you offer across all your channels of communication. This will enhance your audience's trust in the product or service you provide.

Say what you mean and mean what you say.

A strong brand provides a memorable experience for the audience; it makes them feel something. People always remember how experiences make them feel.

When you build your customer base, ensure you do what you promise you will deliver – your aim is to build a network of followers who trust and believe in your brand.

And don't forget – word of mouth is a powerful form of advertising.

A positive approach to handling your finances

Carving out a portfolio career is a lifestyle choice that gives you a chance to generate multiple sources of income. This is a popular choice for many entrepreneurs in the early stages of launching their startup, as it can relieve some financial pressures.

Work out your business plan and financial forecast early on. This is important to ensure long-term sustainability and will enable you to understand every aspect of how your business functions. You don't need to work this out alone – ask for help. It could be a friend or family member with a specialty in this area, or you could research if there are business advisers in your local town or city who can support you.

Start small. Your set-up costs can be minimal
– simply think about what you really need.

Suggestions for starting out:

- a good looking business logo
- engaging written copy about your business
- interesting visuals (whether that's photography, video or both if you have the budget)
- an online presence

Social media channels are free and straightforward
to set up if you can't afford a website at the beginning.
Building your following is key and a great way to test out
your ideas, products and services with your
target audience.

When people visit a website or social media page, you have around 6-8 seconds to grab their attention[†] and keep them engaged. Think about the key message you want to get across in this space of time.

What will encourage the user to find out more?

†Statistic taken from Tribute Media

Every business needs some form of investment and in this digital age, strong branding and design that makes you stand out in your industry is arguably the most important investment you can make.

Manage your expectations in the first year and approach it as an investment in your business. Embrace the progress and changes, and above all else, be kind to yourself.

If you choose to invest your own money, take time to figure out how much money you're willing to lose in the short-term before going ahead with your investment. This will help you plan accordingly and avoid unexpected surprises.

When using the term 'lose', this means that it may feel like a loss at the time. However, it's important to look at it as an investment while you're building momentum, with the aim to make a return on your investment in the future.

Risk-taking can lead to amazing opportunities.
To ensure you maintain your mental wellbeing, with
each opportunity it's important to assess each risk and
possible outcomes in advance.

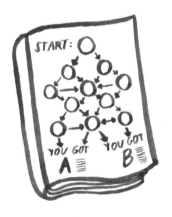

By taking calculated risks, you determine each
eventuality and what you're comfortable with.
Mentally prepare yourself in advance of the outcome.

Remember that it takes time to build financial success, particularly when you're starting at the very beginning.

It's also important to remind yourself that success comes in many forms; it isn't just about financial success. Embrace each achievement and acknowledge the results of your efforts along the way, big and small.

Chapter Three:
Managing your relationships

Your support network

Be true to yourself and surround yourself with positive,
like-minded people. Engage with others who share
similar values and outlooks on life.

One way to grow your support network is to research local networking events. The entrepreneurial lifestyle can feel lonely, so attending regular events is a great way to keep engaged in the industry and surrounded by encouragement and inspiration.

Maintaining a positive and nurturing environment for yourself is key to your personal and professional development, and will help keep you motivated.

Build a reliable, supportive network of people who you trust and who will encourage your ambitions.

Your tribe will enable you to thrive.

Be selective about whose advice you take on board – a lot of contradicting pieces of advice from a wide range of people can become confusing. Aim to seek out guidance from a core group of people who understand the lifestyle you lead and can offer support from experience.

Seeking support from mentors and qualified coaches can be an invaluable part of your network. Think about the areas you need support with and the kind of people who could help with those needs. Who are your peers in your industry? Could you approach them about coaching you on your journey? Is there anyone you admire in your life who could offer guidance based on their experience?

As your success grows, keep people close who are genuine, authentic and supportive of your ambitions – this will keep you grounded, focused and remind you of what's important in life.

Surrounding yourself with people who believe in your vision, support you and understand your lifestyle is so important – not just for your emotional wellbeing, but to also ensure accountability.

An authentic, positive support network guides you with your best interests at heart.

Research has shown that when your actions are accountable to someone or a group of people, you're more likely to achieve your best results[†]. Think about who in your life can hold you accountable to your actions to ensure you keep on track with your goals.

[†]Research taken from omp.gov

The power of networking

Never underestimate the power of networking and where one conversation can lead. Keep your eyes and ears open to new opportunities and take advantage of the chance to demonstrate your ability and experience to your peers.

Recommended reading:
'New To Networking? No Problem. Build your networking skills – one step at a time' at
www.entrepreneur.com/article/204186

In advance of any networking opportunity, think about the value you offer others and what specific opportunities you're looking for. When it comes to doing business with others, it's essential that their cause complements your vision.

Recommended viewing:
Casey Brown's TED Talk,
'Know your worth, and then ask for it'

People buy into people – there's no one like you
so remember that being yourself goes a long way.
Be confident, speak up about what you believe in
and be aware of your body language when
communicating with others.

Recommended viewing:
Amy Cuddy's TED Talk,
'Your Body Language May Shape Who You Are'

Who you choose to associate yourself with speaks volumes about you and your brand. Ensure you collaborate with individuals and businesses whose brands align nicely with the values of your business.

Recommended viewing:
Tony Robbins' TED Talk, *'Why we do what we do'*

Think about your current network and the kind of people you're looking to collaborate with – who can help propel your business to the next level?

When forging new relationships, the conversation must feel mutual rather than one-sided. You ought to each share a genuine interest in one another's ambitions and ask engaging questions.

Recommended viewing:
Susan Cain's TED Talk, *'The power of introverts'*

If you make a connection with someone, discuss how you may mutually work together to collaborate on new ideas, with the aim to strengthen both your brands.

When you make valuable connections at networking events remember to follow up soon after you've met them, while you're still fresh in their minds. Rather than wait for them to contact you, you'll make a very positive impression if you follow up and demonstrate your commitment.

The value of partnerships

A positive partnership enables individuals and organisations that share similar values to collaborate on a mission they feel passionate about. It provides an opportunity to strengthen your brand presence, enhance credibility and broaden your network.

Recommended reading:
Eric Ries' book, *The Lean Startup*

Not all partnerships necessarily require a long-term investment, depending on the circumstances and nature of your business. For example, you might just need a partner or partners for a one-off project. You'll work out whether you need a short or a long-term partnership when the opportunity arises.

Consider what the mutual benefit is for a partnership arrangement – if an organisation is willing to invest their time and resources in you, what's in it for them? Remember there must be a two-way benefit for long-term success.

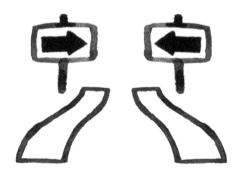

Financial investment aside, what values do you want a potential sponsor or investor to have that align with your business values? Is there a particular aspect, quality or successful outcome in their business that you admire and believe would complement the goal of your business?

With any formal partnership, ensure everything is agreed in writing. This will serve as an important reference point for both parties to ensure that each one delivers what is expected from the outset.

If you feel the partnership is becoming one-sided or there is a lack of communication, have an honest, open conversation about it with your partner. There could be a misunderstanding or the arrangement you'd agreed is not being met. As long as your communication is clear and respectful, you'll work out how best to move things forward.

Recommended reading:
'The Ladder of Inference' at
www.mindtools.com/pages/article/newtmc_91.htm

Don't be afraid to walk away from a partnership or another professional relationship that no longer serves the best interests of your business. There is no need to force a relationship that lacks chemistry, respect or mutual benefits.

If, for whatever reason, an investment or sponsorship proposal doesn't work out the way you'd expected, remember you'll always learn something from the experience.

All positive collaborations are important, however big or small. Each one adds value in different ways and contributes to broadening your reach in the market.

Recommended reading:
Daniel Priestley's book, *Key Person of Influence*.

Conclusion

My story isn't especially unique. I've launched different businesses, gone through trial and error, found out what works and what doesn't, been knocked back, picked myself up again and started over. I've persisted through highly challenging times but, as a result, the rewards that have followed couldn't have tasted sweeter.

I struggled with my mental health in the early years of my business, particularly with anxiety. This affected my wellbeing to the extent that I had to take time out of work to recover and get myself back on track. I made a commitment to myself to overcome and learn from the challenges I faced.

Over time, I entered a much healthier place and learnt how to manage feelings of anxiety, uncertainty and overwhelm – and most importantly, I learnt how to avoid burning out.

This is the side to the entrepreneurial lifestyle, which, it could be argued, doesn't get enough exposure. I'm the first to encourage anyone with a dream for creating their own business to go for it with all their heart – it's an incredible journey, and certainly teaches you so much about yourself, your purpose and what's important to you. But there's no doubt about it – it has its challenges.

Of course, the experience of being an entrepreneur varies and some people may find it more challenging than others – it's not something that is easily quantifiable, by any means. But a common theme that runs through most, if not all, entrepreneur success stories is that running your own business will test your persistence, resilience and adaptability. It requires you step outside of your comfort zone into unchartered territory and to take a leap of faith. There will inevitably be knock-backs, but you'll learn to feel comfortable with being uncomfortable.

After all, if this were an easy path then everyone would be walking it. I like to think of it as more of a squiggly maze, where you're navigating dead ends to find new possibilities until you finally discover the path that leads you to your next step.

I mentor many entrepreneurs on their business journey. Some feel overwhelmed by the process and rather stuck in their business, while others are living with mental health concerns, not sharing this with their friends or family and trying to put on a professional front every day.

These experiences are more common than you might realise and is the inspiration behind my company Calmer – a platform that supports entrepreneurs with managing their mental health and wellbeing while running a business.

I feel it's important to mention that despite what I've outlined, I wouldn't be where I am today if I didn't love what I do. Being an entrepreneur and supporting others on their business journey is my passion, and I truly wouldn't have it any other way. For me, the rewards far outweigh any challenges and the whole experience has made me who I am today. There's definitely something to be said for the character-building nature of entrepreneurship!

However, I also believe that it's vital to acknowledge the importance of managing your mental health and wellbeing while building a business. I'm dedicated to supporting entrepreneurs to achieve good mental health and a balanced lifestyle, as well as raising awareness of the reality of how many people's lives this affects. Your work and your mission are important, but this shouldn't come at the expense of your own health, in any way.

My story is proof that it's absolutely possible to build a thriving business while nurturing and maintaining your wellbeing at the same time – and I sincerely hope this book helps you achieve that too. Doing things you enjoy, seeing people you love and discovering other goals you want to achieve in life are all valuable experiences to embrace fully, both in business and leisure.

Thank you for taking time to read and embrace this perspective and I wish you all the success you desire throughout your life.

Here's to your inner and outer success.
Tania

About the author

Tania Diggory is the founder and director of Calmer, a platform that supports entrepreneurs with managing their mental health and wellbeing while running a business. As an entrepreneur, Business NLP Practitioner and mental health trainer for Mind, Tania helps entrepreneurs and their teams to achieve their full potential and find a business-life balance through delivering workshops, events and mentoring programmes. Her approach has resulted in a range of powerful case studies.

After graduating with a first class honours degree in Modern Drama and Creative Writing from Brunel University, Tania began her career as a professional actress and dancer before launching her own dance school in 2010. Over time, she grew her company from running local classes to producing international events and festivals, involving creative direction, developing partnerships, fundraising and managing large teams of people.

Tania has also supported small and large charities with marketing and creative project management around arts in health initiatives, and embeds dance for wellbeing as part of her workshop approach to enhancing physical, emotional and psychological health.

Tania's mission is to help raise awareness of the challenges entrepreneurs can face and how to manage feelings of anxiety, uncertainty and overwhelm effectively, so they can thrive in their business and in life.

thisiscalmer.com
@thisiscalmer